Envision It! | Handbook

Reading
STREET

Grade **1**

PEARSON

Glenview, Illinois • Boston, Massachusetts
Chandler, Arizona • Upper Saddle River, New Jersey

ISBN-13: 978-0-328-58084-2
ISBN-10:   0-328-58084-8
8 9 10 11 12 V3NL 18 17 16 15 14

Envision It! | Handbook

A note to you!

Peek inside the *Envision It! Handbook* to find lessons, pictures, and charts that will help you become a better reader! You can use it on your own. You can use it with a partner. You can use it in a small group with your teacher.

A note to your teacher. . .

The *Envision It! Handbook* will help your students learn more about comprehension strategies, comprehension skills, vocabulary, and genres. You can use it in small groups to enhance your reading instruction, or students can use it on their own or with a partner to guide their reading.

The *Envision It! Handbook* is filled with lessons, illustrations, photographs, and charts that will help your students become better readers!

Envision It! | Handbook

Contents

Envision It! | Visual Strategies

Background Knowledge

Important Ideas

Inferring

Monitor and Clarify

Predict and Set Purpose

Questioning

Story Structure

Summarize

Text Structure

Visualize

Let's **Think** About...

Comprehension Strategies

As you read,
- think about what you know.
- think about what you want to know.

Comprehension strategies are ways to think about reading. Using a strategy will help you understand what you read.

Ready to **Try** It?

Background Knowledge

Let's **Think** About **Reading!**

- What do I already know?
- What does this remind me of?

Background Knowledge
Mole and the Baby Bird
by Marjorie Newman

I know some things about birds.

Wild birds fly anywhere they want.

Birds in cages can't fly.

Important Ideas

Read Together

> This is important information.

GIANT PANDA

Let's Think About Reading!

- What is important to know?

Important Ideas
A Trip to Washington, D.C.
by Elizabeth Fitzgerald Howard

This is what I learned about Washington, D.C.
Laws are made there.

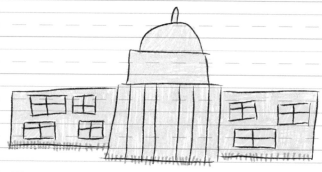

The President lives and works there in
the White House.

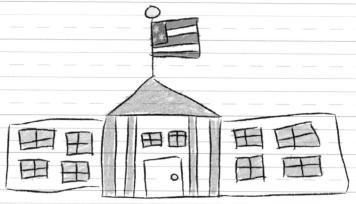

There are many flags in Washington.
The flag stands for America.

Inferring

Let's Think About Reading!

- What do I already know?
- How does what I know help me understand?

Inferring
Ruby in Her Own Time
by Jonathan Emmett

I think Father Duck was worried about Ruby. He asked lots of questions.

Will it ever hatch?

Will she ever eat?

Will she ever swim?

Ruby was fine. She grew up in her own time.

11

Monitor and Clarify

Let's **Think** About **Reading!**

- What does not make sense?
- How can I fix it?

Monitor and Clarify
Mama's Birthday Present
by Carmen Tafolla

<u>Mama's Birthday Present</u> is about a surprise party.

<u>What I didn't understand</u>	<u>What I did to help myself</u>
What's a confetti egg?	I read the page again. I also looked at the picture. I saw hollow egg shells. I saw paper, glue, and paint.
Why was Francisco sad at the party?	I kept reading to find out. He was sad because he didn't have a present for Mama.

The story ended with Mama being happy about the party. Francisco's present was the party!

Predict and Set Purpose

Let's **Think** About **Reading!**

- What do I already know?
- What do I think will happen?
- What do I want to learn?

Predict and Set Purpose
A Big Fish for Max
by Rosemary Wells

Read Together

I read <u>A Big Fish for Max</u> for fun.

I didn't think Max would get a fish.

My prediction was right.
Max didn't get a fish.

Grandma, Max, and Ruby went to
the fish store and got a fish to eat.

Questioning

Why is it cracked?

Let's **Think** About **Reading!**

- What questions do I have?

Questioning
Honey Bees
by Jesús Cervantes

Honey Bees tells about bees. This is what I wanted to find out.

Are all bees the same?
What happens in the hive?
What is a hive made of?

I found the answers. Now I have a new question. How do we get the honey away from the bees?

Honey

Story Structure

Beginning

Middle

End

Let's Think About Reading!

- What happens in the beginning?
- What happens in the middle?
- What happens in the end?

Story Structure
Peter's Chair
by Ezra Jack Keats

Peter's Chair is about a boy. He does not want to share his things with his new baby sister.

Beginning: Peter is sad. Everybody is fussing over his new baby sister.

Middle: Peter runs away. He takes his chair. He doesn't want his sister to have it.

End: Peter goes home. He helps paint his chair pink for his sister.

19

Summarize

The dog knocked over the table.

Let's Think About Reading!

- What happens in the story?
- What is the story mostly about?

Summarize
Pig in a Wig
by Susan Stevens Crummel

<u>Pig in a Wig</u> is a silly story. Pig eats too much and gets sick. She gets medicine. Then Max and Pam play music. Pig does a jig.

happy pig

sick pig

dancing pig

Text Structure

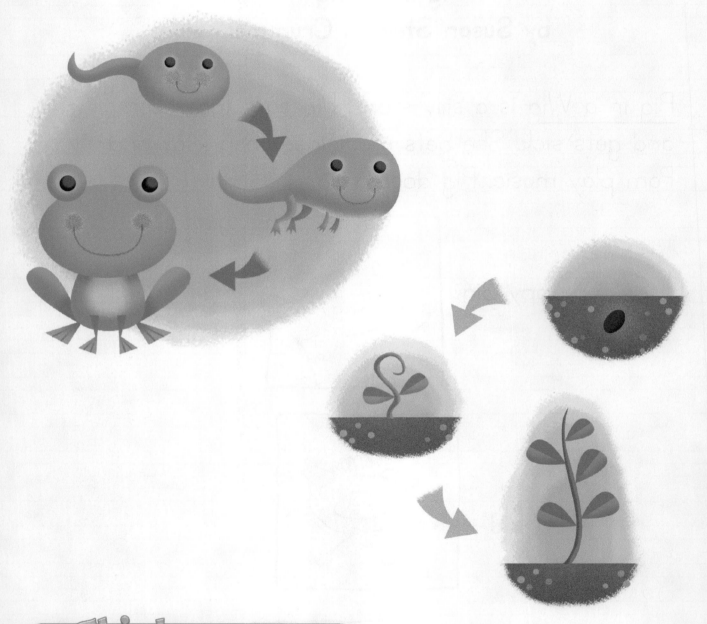

Let's **Think** About **Reading!**

- How is the story organized?
- Are there any patterns?

Text Structure
I'm a Caterpillar
by Jean Marzollo

I'm a Caterpillar tells how a caterpillar turns into a butterfly. This is how.

First, it's a caterpillar.

Next, it becomes a pupa.

Then it's a chrysalis.

Finally, it's a butterfly!

Butterflies lay eggs. Guess what hatches from them? Caterpillars!

Visualize

Let's Think About Reading!

• What pictures do I see in my mind?

Visualize
Frog and Toad Together
by Arnold Lobel

<u>Frog and Toad Together</u> is about planting seeds. I had a picture in my head. Toad was yelling at his seeds. In my head, the seeds had faces, arms, and legs. They were holding their ears under the ground. That picture made me laugh.

Making pictures helps me understand what I read. Toad didn't understand that seeds need sun and rain to grow.

Envision It! | Visual Skills

Let's Think About...

Read Together

Comprehension Skills

As you read,
- think about how the story is like or unlike other stories you have read.
- think about what happens and why it happens.
- use the pictures to help you.

Comprehension skills will help you understand what you read.

Ready to Try It? ▶

Realism and Fantasy

Realism

Fantasy

How to Identify Realism and Fantasy

Realism tells a story as it might happen in real life. Fantasy is not like real life.

See It!

- Look at pages 28–29. What do you see? Look at the words. What is the difference between the two pictures?

- Think of movies where animals can talk. Close your eyes and picture the movie in your mind. If animals and objects can talk like people, the movie is not realistic—it is a fantasy.

Say It!

- Tell a story about the bears. Does the story seem like something that could happen in real life?

Do It!

- Look through some books. Which stories are realistic, and which stories are fantasy? Your teacher can help you decide.

Objectives

● Distinguish the difference between a realistic story and a fantasy. ● Use what you already know to better understand what you are reading.

Envision It! | Skill Strategy

Skill

Strategy

READING STREET ONLINE
ENVISION IT! ANIMATIONS
www.ReadingStreet.com

Comprehension Skill

Realism and Fantasy

- A realistic story is one that could happen in real life. A fantasy is a story that could never happen in real life.

- Clues that tell you a story is a fantasy could be animals talking, animals wearing clothes, or people doing activities such as flying.

Comprehension Strategy

Background Knowledge

As you read, use what you already know about what you are reading to help you understand.

32

Liza's Favorite Book

Before dinner, Liza sat on the floor in her room and read her favorite book. The book was called Bears. It was about a family of bears who lived near a cool stream.

Liza loved learning about bears and other animals. She had two pets of her own—a cat named Smudge and a goldfish named Swimmy. She loved watching Smudge chase his jingle toy. And she loved watching Swimmy flip her little fins.

Since Liza didn't have a pet bear to watch, she thought the best way to learn about them would be to read about them. She hoped one day her mom and dad would take her to the zoo.

Strategy What do you already know about animals that helped you understand this paragraph?

Skill What are some clues that helped you figure out if this story is realistic or a fantasy?

Your Turn!

Need a Review?
See *Envision It!* Skills and Strategies for more help.

Ready to Try It?
As you read other text, use what you learned about realism and fantasy, and background knowledge, to help you understand it.

Comprehension Skill

Realism and Fantasy

- A realistic story is a made-up story about things that can really happen. A fantasy is a made-up story about things that can't really happen.

- In a realistic story, the characters in it do and say things like the people you know.

- In a fantasy, the characters, the setting, the things that happen, or a combination of these things are magical or fantastical.

Comprehension Strategy

Questioning

Questioning is asking good questions about important text. Ask questions before, during, and after you read.

Three Bears

Once upon a time there were three bears—Mama Bear, Papa Bear, and their son, Cubby. The Bear Family lived in a small cottage in a thick forest.

One morning, after the three bears all got dressed, Papa Bear made some delicious hot cereal for breakfast. The hot cereal was called porridge.

"When our porridge is cool," Mama Bear said, "we should eat it up quickly. I heard about a girl named Goldilocks who likes to visit cottages and eat up all the porridge in the kitchen. We don't want that to happen to us!"

Strategy What if you didn't know what a cottage is? What questions could you ask to find out?

Skill What did you read in this paragraph that tells you this story is a fantasy?

Your Turn!

 Need a Review?
See *Envision It!* Skills and Strategies for more help.

▶ **Ready to Try It?**
As you read other text, use what you learned about realism and fantasy, and questioning, to help you understand it.

Literary Elements

Characters

BROTHER

MOMMY

DADDY

SISTER

Setting

Plot

Beginning

Middle

End

Theme

How to Identify Literary Elements

Stories have characters, a setting, a plot, and a theme.

See It!

- Look at the picture on pages 36–37. What happens in the beginning, middle, and end of the story? Who are the characters? What is the setting?

Say It!

- Look at pages 36–37. Retell the story that you see on page 37 to a partner.

- Now think about the "big idea," or theme, of the story on page 37. Tell a partner what you think the theme is.

Do It!

- After reading, make a list of what happened first, next, and last in the story. This is the plot.

- Draw a picture of the characters or setting of a story you are reading.

Envision It! | Skill Strategy

Skill

Strategy

READING STREET ONLINE
ENVISION IT! ANIMATIONS
www.ReadingStreet.com

Comprehension Skill

Character, Setting, Plot, and Theme

- Character, setting, plot, and theme are called literary elements.

- A character is a person or animal in a story.

- The setting of a story is when and where the story takes place.

- The plot of a story is what happens in it.

- The theme of a story is its "big idea."

Comprehension Strategy

Summarize

To summarize a story, tell a few sentences about what happens in it. Think about what the characters do.

After a Picnic

One evening, the Bunny Family walked home from a picnic. Brother and Sister were so tired that they fell asleep in Mommy and Daddy's arms.

Mommy and Daddy put Brother and Sister to bed and tiptoed out. But Brother and Sister had slept so long after the picnic that they weren't tired anymore.

Skill What is the plot of this story?

"Don't you wish we could go on picnics every day?" whispered Sister.

"Yes," said Brother, "I had such a good time eating good food and playing tag."

Strategy Summarize the story. Remember to only use a few sentences.

Brother and Sister talked quietly a little bit longer, but they knew they had to fall asleep soon so they could wake up in time for school in the morning.

Your Turn!

Ⅱ Need a Review?
See *Envision It!* Skills and Strategies for more help.

▷ Ready to Try It?
As you read other text, use what you learned about literary elements and summarize to help you understand it.

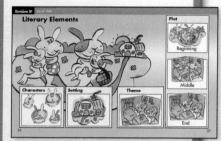

Skill

Strategy

Comprehension Skill

Character, Setting, Plot, and Theme

- A character is a person or animal in a story. You can describe reasons for the way a character feels.

- The setting of a story is when and where the story takes place.

- The plot of a story is made up of a problem and a solution.

- Sometimes a story's theme, or "big idea," is a lesson.

Comprehension Strategy

Predict and Set Purpose

Deciding why you will read something is called setting a purpose for reading. Thinking about what will happen next in a story is called predicting. Confirm the predictions you make by "reading the part that tells."

Downtown Picnic

"Let's go on a picnic!" Sofia called.

Sofia and her little brother, Patrick, were all set. Sofia had a basket filled with grapes, juice boxes, and crackers. Patrick had a blanket draped across his arm.

But Mom said there wasn't time for a picnic. They lived on the tenth floor of a tall apartment building downtown, and it would take too long to ride the elevator to the first floor and walk to the park.

Sofia and Patrick were sad. But Mom had an idea. "Why don't we have a picnic out on our balcony?" she suggested. "We'll sit on the blanket and eat our snacks there. We have time to do that."

"Great idea!" said Sofia and Patrick. Now they were happy.

Skill Why are Sofia and Patrick sad?

Strategy Did you predict that the family would have a picnic on their balcony? Why or why not?

Your Turn!

⏸ Need a Review?
See *Envision It!* Skills and Strategies for more help.

▶ Ready to Try It?
As you read other text, use what you learned about literary elements, and predict and set purpose, to help you understand it.

43

Cause and Effect

Cause

Effect

How to Identify Cause and Effect

A cause tells why something happened. An effect is what happened.

See It!

- Look for clue words in a text, such as *because, so, since,* and *then.* They can tell about cause and effect.
- Look at page 44. What happened to the snowman? Why?

Say It!

- To understand cause and effect, ask yourself, "What happened?" and "Why did this happen?"
- Take turns telling a partner what happened in a story, and how it happened.

Do It!

- Imagine that it starts to rain while you are at the park. Write what you would do next.
- Make a graphic organizer that helps you figure out cause and effect.

EFFECT What happened	CAUSE Why it happened

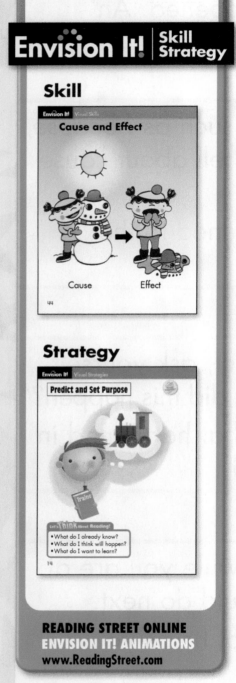

Envision It! Skill Strategy

Skill

Cause and Effect

Cause | Effect

Strategy

Predict and Set Purpose

Let's Think About Reading!
- What do I already know?
- What do I think will happen?
- What do I want to learn?

Comprehension Skill

Cause and Effect

- An effect is what happens. A cause is why it happens.

- Words such as *because, so,* and *since* can help you figure out why something happens.

Comprehension Strategy

Predict and Set Purpose

Before you read something, think about why you're going to read it. What do you think will happen? What do you think will happen next?

A Snowman

One sunny winter day, Jadyn went outside and rolled three little balls of snow across the backyard until they were three big balls of snow. Then she placed them on top one another. She was making a snowman!

Jadyn used a hat, a scarf, a carrot, and coal to make the snowman look more like a person. It was as tall as she was.

Later that day, Jadyn was excited to go see her snowman again. Maybe she would make a friend for it. But when she went outside, her snowman was gone! It had melted because of the hot sun.

Jadyn decided that she'd make a new snowman on a cloudier day.

Strategy What do you think will happen to Jadyn's snowman? Why do you think so?

Skill Why did the snowman melt? What clue word helped you know?

Your Turn!

 Need a Review?
See *Envision It!* Skills and Strategies for more help.

Ready to Try It?
As you read other text, use what you learned about cause and effect, and predict and set purpose, to help you understand it.

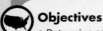

Objectives
- Determine cause and effect in text.
- Use sensory details to understand text.

Skill

Strategy

Comprehension Skill

Cause and Effect

- As you read, look for what happened and why it happened.

- Sometimes an effect can have more than one cause.

- Sometimes a cause can have more than one effect.

Comprehension Strategy

Visualize

As you read, create pictures in your mind to better understand how something looks, sounds, feels, tastes, or smells.

Blizzards

A blizzard is a very bad snowstorm with strong winds and cold temperatures. Blizzards happen when warm air and polar air meet.

It is hard to see very far in a blizzard because there is so much blowing snow. This makes it dangerous to drive a car or even to walk.

The heavy winds of a blizzard can damage power lines and knock down trees. If a person is outside during a blizzard, the cold air can cause him or her to get frostbite.

Skill What are two effects caused by the heavy winds of a blizzard?

The worst blizzard in the United States was in 1949, when it snowed heavily for seven weeks in a row!

Strategy What did you visualize as you read "Blizzards"?

Your Turn!

Need a Review?
See *Envision It!* Skills and Strategies for more help.

Ready to Try It?
As you read other text, use what you learned about cause and effect, and visualize, to help you understand it.

Main Idea and Details

Main Idea

Details

How to Identify Main Idea and Details

The main idea is what a story is all about. Details tell more about the main idea.

See It!

- Look at page 50. What is the main idea of the picture? What are the details?

- Look at illustrations to help you figure out the main idea of a story. What do the pictures tell you?

Say It!

- The main idea of a story is what the story is mostly about. After reading, tell a partner what you think the main idea is. Why do you think so?

- Ask a partner: "Does my main idea make sense?"

Do It!

- Use a web like the one below to identify the main idea of a story.

- Read this main idea: *Mary plays at the park.* What does Mary do there? Write a sentence giving details about what Mary does at the park.

Objectives
• Identify main idea and supporting details in text. • Determine which ideas in text are important.

Envision It! | Skill Strategy

Skill

Strategy

Comprehension Skill

Main Idea and Details

• The main idea of an article is what the article is all about.

• Details are pieces of information that tell more about the main idea.

Comprehension Strategy

Important Ideas

Some things you read are more important than other things you read. Focus on information that matters, not bits of information that don't help you understand what you're reading.

52

At the Grocery Store

A grocery store is a store where people go to buy food and other household items.

Each aisle in the store has different types of things. Flour and sugar are in the baking aisle. Bagels and hotdog buns are in the bread aisle.

Skill What is the main idea of this paragraph? What are some details?

People who are just buying a few items use a basket. People who are buying food for a week or more use a cart. Moms and dads might let their kids sit in the front of the cart. Older kids help their parents shop.

Strategy Is the last sentence in this paragraph an important idea? Why or why not?

Some grocery stores are open all night! It's funny to think that while you are sound asleep, someone is at the grocery store, trying to decide what kind of cheese to buy.

Your Turn!

Need a Review?
See *Envision It!* Skills and Strategies for more help.

Ready to Try It?
As you read other text, use what you learned about main idea and details, and important ideas, to help you understand it.

Envision It! | Skill Strategy

Skill

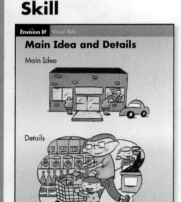

Strategy

Comprehension Skill

Main Idea and Details

• The main idea of a story is what the story is all about.

• When you read a story, ask yourself what the main idea is. Then look for details that support your answer.

Comprehension Strategy

Story Structure

Stories are arranged in a sequence from beginning to end. One event in a story leads to the next event.

Shopping List

Tory went with her older sister, Jane, to the grocery store. Mom had asked them if they would go there to pick up a few things for dinner.

Tory and Jane got a shopping cart and filled it with all the things from Mom's list. But when they got to the last item on the list, they were confused.

"The last thing says potatoes," said Jane, "but it doesn't say what kind. Could she mean raw potatoes?"

"Or a box of potato flakes?" asked Tory. "Or frozen hashed brown potatoes?"

Jane pulled out her cell phone and called Mom to find out. "Mom changed her mind," Jane told Tory. "She wants rice instead."

cereal
bread
milk
eggs
potatoes

Strategy How does what happens in the beginning of this story lead to Jane calling Mom?

Skill What is the main idea of "Shopping List"? What details support the main idea?

Your Turn!

 Need a Review?
See *Envision It!* Skills and Strategies for more help.

▶ **Ready to Try It?**
As you read other text, use what you learned about main idea and details, and story structure, to help you understand it.

Author's Purpose

Inform

Entertain

How to Find Author's Purpose

Authors write to inform or to entertain.

See It!

- Before you read, look at the pictures. What do you see? How do the pictures make you feel? Why do you think they were chosen?

- Look at page 56. Read the words. What do the words and pictures tell you about the author's purpose?

Say It!

- Listen to a story. What kinds of words does the author use? Do the words make it sound like the author is trying to entertain you or teach you something?

Do It!

- Write the author's important ideas. Then read what you wrote. What is the author trying to tell you?

- Write a story about eating lunch with a friend. Before you start your story, decide whether you want it to entertain or inform readers.

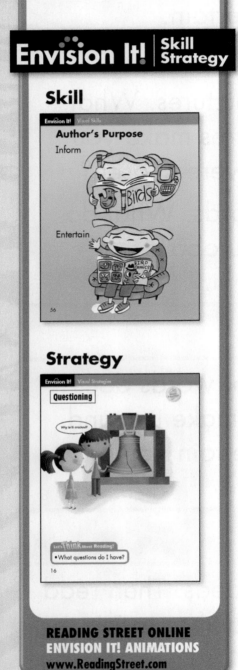

Envision It! | Skill Strategy

Skill

Envision It! Visual Skills

Author's Purpose

Inform

Entertain

56

Strategy

Envision It! Visual Strategies

Questioning

Why is it cracked?

Let's THINK About Reading!
• What questions do I have?

16

READING STREET ONLINE
ENVISION IT! ANIMATIONS
www.ReadingStreet.com

Comprehension Skill

Author's Purpose

- The author's purpose is the reason an author wrote a story or article.

- An author writes to give information or to entertain.

Comprehension Strategy

Questioning

As you read, think about the questions you have. Where can you find the answers?

 **Birds**

A bird is an animal that has feathers, wings, and a beak. All birds hatch from eggs, and most can fly.

There are many kinds of birds. Some, such as hummingbirds and sparrows, are small. Some, such as swans and peacocks, are big. Some have very colorful feathers and some do not.

Strategy What questions do you have after reading this sentence? Where can you find the answers?

Different kinds of birds eat different things. They can eat seeds, berries, insects, fruit, nectar, meat, or plants.

Different kinds of birds make different noises too. Ducks quack, geese honk, and songbirds sing beautiful songs.

Skill Why do you think the author wrote "Birds"?

Your Turn!

⏸ **Need a Review?**
See *Envision It!* Skills and Strategies for more help.

▷ **Ready to Try It?**
As you read other text, use what you learned about author's purpose and questioning to help you understand it.

Skill

Strategy

Comprehension Skill

Author's Purpose

• An author always has a purpose, or reason, for writing.

• Sometimes an author writes for more than one reason.

• Looking at the pictures in a story can help you decide what the author's purpose is.

Comprehension Strategy

Monitor and Clarify

If you don't understand something you are reading, use what you already know about the topic to help clear up your confusion.

60

Bunko Bird

Bunko Bird was excited! This was the day he was going to try to fly. He put on his silly hat and stood at the edge of the nest.

"Watch me fly!" Bunko chirped.

But his little legs wouldn't move. He was too nervous. The bright blue sky suddenly seemed gray and scary.

"I can't do it!" Bunko chirped.

Just then Bunko saw a tiny chickadee fly through the sky, land on a tree branch, and sing a little song. "If that tiny bird can fly," chirped Bunko, "so can I!"

And he stepped out of the nest, into the open, and flew through the bright blue sky.

Strategy Did you read something you don't understand? Use what you know about birds to "fix up" your understanding.

Skill Why do you think the author wrote "Bunko Bird"?

Your Turn!

 Need a Review?
See *Envision It!* Skills and Strategies for more help.

Ready to Try It?
As you read other text, use what you learned about compare and contrast, and monitor and clarify, to help you understand it.

Compare and Contrast

How to Compare and Contrast

During reading, we compare and contrast by thinking about what is alike and what is different.

See It!

- Look at the picture on page 62. What do you see? What is alike? What is different?

- Look at things around the classroom. What things are alike? What things are different? Make a list of the things you see that are alike and different.

Say It!

- Name an object in the classroom. Have a partner tell you one thing in the classroom that is similar to that object, and one thing that is different.

Do It!

- Draw a Venn diagram. Use it to compare and contrast two things in nature. Then draw them. Write captions that tell how the things are alike or different.

Skill

Strategy

Comprehension Skill

Compare and Contrast

- When you compare, you tell how two or more things are alike.

- When you contrast, you tell how they are different.

- Words such as *alike, both, different,* and *same* can help you compare and contrast.

Comprehension Strategy

Monitor and Clarify

If you don't understand something you are reading, go back and read that part again. It might make sense the second time.

Apples & Oranges

James was hungry. Mom told James, "Take one piece of fruit for a snack."

James went to the kitchen. On the table there was an apple and an orange. James could not decide which piece of fruit he wanted to eat.

He looked at the fruit. How were the apple and the orange alike? They were both about the same size. They were both round.

But their colors were different. The apple was red and the orange was—well, orange! The apple felt smooth and the orange felt bumpy.

James picked up the apple and bit into it. "I will eat the orange later," he said.

Skill These sentences tell how the apple and orange are alike. What clue words are used to compare?

Strategy Did you understand how the apple and the orange are different? If not, read this paragraph again.

Your Turn!

Need a Review?
See *Envision It!* Skills and Strategies for more help.

Ready to Try It?
As you read other text, use what you learned about compare and contrast, and monitor and clarify, to help you understand it.

Skill

Strategy

Comprehension Skill

Compare and Contrast

- When you compare and contrast, you tell how two or more things are alike or different.

- You can also compare and contrast ideas or stories.

- Using a graphic organizer like the Venn diagram below can help you compare and contrast.

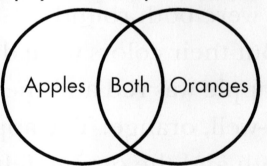

Apples   Both   Oranges

Comprehension Strategy

Summarize

When you summarize an article, think about what it is mostly about. Use your own words to give a short description.

66

Not Yet Picked

Fruit is the part of a tree, bush, or vine that has seeds in it and is good to eat. Apples and oranges are both fruit. Have you tasted them?

Apple trees grow in an orchard. Orange trees grow in a grove. Apples grow best where it is not too hot or too cold. Unlike apples, oranges grow best in very warm places.

Orange blossoms, or flowers, are white. Apple blossoms are also white, but most have a pink tint. The orange blossom is the state flower of Florida, and the apple blossom is the state flower of Michigan and Arkansas. Why do you think these states chose tree blossoms to be their state flower?

Skill What would you write in a Venn diagram to compare and contrast the information in this paragraph?

Strategy Use your own words to summarize what you read.

Your Turn!

⏸ Need a Review?
See *Envision It!* Skills and Strategies for more help.

▷ Ready to Try It?
As you read other text, use what you learned about compare and contrast, and summarize, to help you understand it.

Sequence

How to Identify Sequence

The sequence is the order in which things happen in a story—what happens first, next, and last.

See It!

- Look at the picture on page 68. Follow the arrows that show the order of events. What happens first, next, and last? Tell this sequence to a partner.

Say It!

- Tell a partner how you got ready for school in the morning, in order of what happened first, next, and last.

Do It!

- Make a sequence diagram like the one below to help you keep track of how you tie your shoe.

First	Next	Last

Envision It! | Skill Strategy

Skill

Strategy

Comprehension Skill

Sequence

- Sequence is the order of events in a story.

- Clue words such as *first, next, last, then,* and *finally* can help you figure out the sequence.

Comprehension Strategy

Visualize

As you read, think of the pictures that are in your mind. Authors often use descriptive words to help you understand what you're reading.

Lucky and Rafe

Rafe's dog, Lucky, is a year old. Rafe thinks about the past year.

First, Rafe's parents take him to the animal shelter. They all walk inside, make their way across the tile floor, and enter a room in the back. Three puppies wiggle in a blue box. Rafe chooses the puppy with the tan patch on his eye. He names the puppy Lucky.

Then Lucky grows. So does Rafe. Lucky enjoys running after sticks and bringing them back to Rafe.

Finally, Lucky turns a year old. When he stands on his back legs, he is almost as tall as Rafe. Now Lucky isn't a puppy anymore—he's a dog. In fact, Lucky is a lucky dog!

Skill What happens after Rafe and his parents walk inside the animal shelter?

Strategy Describe the pictures of the shelter you saw in your mind as you read this paragraph.

Your Turn!

 Need a Review?
See *Envision It!* Skills and Strategies for more help.

Ready to Try It?
As you read other text, use what you learned about sequence and visualize to help you understand it.

Skill

Strategy

Comprehension Skill

Sequence

- Sequence is the order in which things happen in a story or an article.

- Making a time line can help you organize the order of what happens.

- As you read, keep track of what happens first, next, and last.

Comprehension Strategy

Inferring

Inferring is using what you know and what you read to come up with your own ideas. Use evidence from the text to help you infer.

Puppies Grow

You probably already know that a baby dog is called a puppy. When puppies are born, they can't see or hear. Like human babies, they mostly just drink milk and sleep!

In about nine days, puppies' eyes open and they learn to walk. Then, when they are six weeks old, their teeth have formed. Now they drink less milk and can chew solid food.

Skill What do puppies do after they are born?

When puppies are three months old, they eat only solid food. They love to play and explore! At six months old, they are almost as big as their parents.

Strategy Why do you think puppies don't explore when they are first born?

A puppy is an adult dog when it has turned a year old. How old will you be when you're an adult?

Your Turn!

❚❚ Need a Review?
See *Envision It!* Skills and Strategies for more help.

▶ Ready to Try It?
As you read other text, use what you learned about sequence and inferring to help you understand it.

Fact and Opinion

Fact = It is raining.

Opinion = Rainy days are fun!

How to Identify Fact and Opinion

A statement of fact can be proven true or false. A statement of opinion tells someone's ideas or feelings.

See It!

- Look at the pictures on pages 74–75. Read the fact. How can you prove it? Read the opinion. How do you know it is an opinion?
- Look for clue words that might tell if something is an opinion and not a fact. Words like *favorite*, *great*, *exciting*, and *boring* describe someone's beliefs or feelings.

Say It!

- Read the following sentences aloud. Tell which one is a fact and which is an opinion.

1. Gosh, it is so hot in here!
2. The thermometer shows that it is 92 degrees Fahrenheit!

Do It!

- Write two sentences about school. One should tell a fact. One should tell an opinion.
- Use a graphic organizer like the one below to figure out the facts and opinions of a selection.

Facts	Opinions

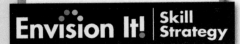

Skill

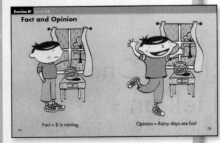

Strategy

READING STREET ONLINE
ENVISION IT! ANIMATIONS
www.ReadingStreet.com

Comprehension Skill

Fact and Opinion

- A statement of fact is something we can prove to be true.

- A statement of opinion is the way someone feels about something.

Comprehension Strategy

Story Structure

Story structure is what happens in the beginning, middle, and end of a story. How is a story put together?

Rainy Day

Read Together

Kyle was about to grab his helmet and go for a bike ride. Then he looked out the window. It was raining.

"I guess I can't go for a bike ride," Kyle told his dad.

"Yes, it's raining hard," said Kyle's dad. "I was going to mow the lawn, but now I can't. I don't like rain, especially on Saturday! What do you want to do on this miserable day?"

"I have a great idea!" Kyle said. "Would you like to play my new computer game with me?"

Kyle's dad said that he would be happy to play the new game. Kyle decided that rainy days are fun!

Strategy
What is the first thing that happens in this story?

Skill What facts can you find in this paragraph? What opinions can you find?

Your Turn!

❙❙ Need a Review?
See *Envision It!* Skills and Strategies for more help.

▶ Ready to Try It?
As you read other text, use what you learned about fact and opinion, and story structure, to help you understand it.

Objectives
- Find facts stated in a text. • Find opinions stated in a text. • Determine which ideas in text are important.

Envision It! | Skill Strategy

Skill

Envision It! Word Skill
Fact and Opinion

Fact = It is raining.

Opinion = Rainy days are fun!

Strategy

Envision It! Visual Strategies

Important Ideas

This is important information.

GIANT PANDA

Let's Think About Reading!
- What is important to know?

8

READING STREET ONLINE
ENVISION IT! ANIMATIONS
www.ReadingStreet.com

Comprehension Skill

Fact and Opinion

- You can prove a statement of fact true or false by checking a book or asking an expert.

- To figure out if a statement is fact or opinion, look for clue words such as *best* and *should*. These words often signal statements of opinions.

Comprehension Strategy

Important Ideas

Deciding if an idea is important or not so important is a key to understanding text. As you read, look for words and phrases that tell about the topic.

80

Rain Forests

Tropical rain forests are beautiful forests with tall trees, hot weather, and a lot of rain. In some rain forests it rains more than an inch every day. Tourists who visit a rain forest must dress properly.

The trees in a rain forest grow closely together. The top layer of branches and leaves of these trees is called the canopy. Many animals live in rain forests, and most of them live in the canopy.

People are cutting down rain forest trees to use for wood and to use the land for farms. But people should not destroy the forests because they are home to so many plants and animals.

Strategy What is an important idea in this paragraph? What is not an important idea?

Skill Which of the sentences in this paragraph is a fact? Which one is an opinion? How do you know?

Your Turn!

Need a Review?
See *Envision It!* Skills and Strategies for more help.

Ready to Try It?
As you read other text, use what you learned about fact and opinion, and important ideas, to help you understand it.

Draw Conclusions

= Happy

How to Draw Conclusions

When we draw conclusions, we form an opinion based on the information.

See It!

- Look at the picture on page 82. What do you see? What conclusion can you make about what is happening?

- Picture in your mind someone who is mad, happy, sad, or excited. What kinds of clues do they give you about their mood?

Say It!

- Tell a partner what you see on page 82. Why is the boy happy?

- Ask questions such as "Why is this happening?" as you read.

Do It!

- Practice drawing conclusions by writing "Who or What Am I?" questions. Give three facts about something, and ask a partner to draw a conclusion based on the facts.

Envision It! | Skill Strategy

Skill

Strategy

Comprehension Skill

Draw Conclusions

- To draw conclusions is to figure out more about the information in an article.

- Use what you have read and what you already know to draw conclusions.

Comprehension Strategy

Text Structure

Text structure is the way an article is organized. Some articles use time-order organization. Look for patterns as you read.

Toys

Boys and girls have played with toys for thousands of years. But they haven't always played with the kinds of toys you may be used to.

For instance, children in ancient times did not play with plastic dolls that had moving eyes and computerized voices. Their dolls might have been carved out of wax or clay.

Skill How real do you think the dolls from ancient times looked?

Children in ancient times did not go to the toy store and buy boxes of construction sets that were filled with plastic blocks. They made buildings out of sticks they found outside.

Strategy What is the text structure of the second and third paragraphs?

Years from now, boys and girls will read about toys you played with and think they are old-fashioned! Toys will always bring a smile to children's faces.

Your Turn!

 Need a Review?
See *Envision It!* Skills and Strategies for more help.

Ready to Try It?
As you read other text, use what you learned about draw conclusions and text structure to help you understand it.

85

Comprehension Skill

Draw Conclusions

• Drawing conclusions is figuring out more about characters and events in a story.

• An author doesn't always tell you everything. When you read, you have to draw conclusions from what the author does tell you.

Comprehension Strategy

Background Knowledge

Background knowledge is what you already know about something. Use background knowledge before, during, and after reading.

Zipp's Toys

Zipp is a furry gray cat who likes playing with toys, but not the kinds of toys you would imagine a cat to like. For instance, one day someone in her family brought her a catnip mouse from the store.

"I don't like catnip mice," meowed Zipp, and she went back to chasing a crumpled piece of paper across the floor.

> **Strategy** What do you already know about cats that helps you understand this sentence?

Another day, someone in her family brought her a feathery ball from the store.

"I don't like feathery balls," meowed Zipp, and she went back to batting a pen cap off the table.

From then on, Zipp's family didn't bring Zipp any toys from the store.

> **Skill** If Zipp's family doesn't bring Zipp any toys from the store, what do you think she will play with?

Your Turn!

 Need a Review?
See *Envision It!* Skills and Strategies for more help.

▶ **Ready to Try It?**
As you read other text, use what you learned about draw conclusions and background knowledge to help you understand it.

Facts and Details

How to Identify Facts and Details

Facts and details give information. Facts are pieces of information. Details help you see what is taking place.

See It!

- Look at page 88. What facts and details do you see? Discuss with a partner.

- Look at pictures from your reading to help find facts and details about a topic.

Say It!

- Look around the room. Pick an object about which you can tell a partner one fact and one or more details.

Do It!

- As you read, use a web like the one below to identify facts and details of what you're reading.

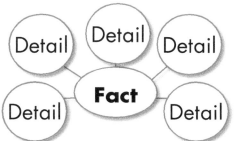

Envision It! | **Skill Strategy**

Skill

Strategy

Comprehension Skill

Facts and Details

• Facts are pieces of information that can be proven true.

• Details can help you see what is taking place in an article.

Comprehension Strategy

Inferring

As you read, think about what you already know. How does this help you understand what you are reading?

90

All About Flowers

A flower is made up of many parts. The part that grows up from the ground is the stem. Leaves grow from the stem.

A head grows from the stem too. This is where the petals are. Petals can be white, pink, yellow, blue, purple, red, orange, or a combination of these colors. There are different sizes and shapes of petals.

Skill What facts and details did you read in this paragraph?

Under the ground are the roots of the flower. Roots soak up water and other things that help the flower grow.

The next time you see a flower, look at it closely. See if you can spot the stem, the leaves, the head, and the petals.

Strategy Why doesn't the author ask you to see if you can spot the roots?

Your Turn!

 Need a Review?
See *Envision It!* Skills and Strategies for more help.

▷ **Ready to Try It?**
As you read other text, use what you learned about facts and details, and inferring, to help you understand it.

Envision It! | Skill Strategy

Skill

Strategy

Comprehension Skill

Facts and Details

• Information about a topic is made up of many facts and details.

• Nonfiction text is filled with facts and details.

• As you read, look for facts. Then look for supporting details.

Comprehension Strategy

Text Structure

An author organizes information in a certain order. As you read, pay attention to the structure of the text.

The Run for the Roses

Every spring in Kentucky since 1874, there is a famous horse race called the Kentucky Derby. In 1904, the red rose became the official flower of this race. Then, in 1932, a flowery tradition began.

The tradition is that each year, more than 400 real roses are sewn into a large green cloth to make a soft garland, or blanket. The garland is placed on the back of the horse that wins the race. Imagine how sweet that garland must smell!

Some people call the Kentucky Derby "The Run for the Roses."

Strategy How did the way the author organized this paragraph help you understand it better?

Skill What facts and details did you read in this paragraph?

Your Turn!

Need a Review?
See *Envision It!* Skills and Strategies for more help.

Ready to Try It?
As you read other text, use what you learned about facts and details, and text structure, to help you understand it.

WORDS! | Vocabulary

Base Words

Context Clues

Antonyms

Synonyms

Prefixes

Suffixes

Dictionary

Thesaurus

Multiple-Meaning Words

Related Words

Compound Words

Let's Think About...

Read Together

Vocabulary Skills and Strategies

As you read,
- think about the parts of a word.
- use clues in words and sentences.
- use a dictionary to help you.

Vocabulary skills and strategies are ways to help you figure out what words mean. This will help you understand what you read.

Ready to Try It?

Base Words

A base word is a word that cannot be broken down into smaller words or word parts. *Appear* and *cloud* are base words.

Appear

Knowing the meaning of a base word can help you understand the meaning of longer words.

Cloud

Context Clues

Read the words before and after a word that you don't know to help you make sense of it.

I saw a robin, a bluebird, a sapsucker, and a turkey while walking in the woods.

Envision It!

Context Clues

Read the words before and after a word that
you don't know to help you make sense of it.

I saw a robin, a bluebird,
a sapsucker, and a turkey
while walking in the woods.

Context Clues

- Context clues are words in the same sentence or nearby sentences that can help you figure out the meaning of a word you don't know.

- As you read, you might come to a word you don't know. Look at the words and sentences near the unknown word to help you figure out the word's meaning.

- As you read "Forests," look for context clues to help you figure out the meaning of a word you don't know.

Forests

There are two main kinds of forests: deciduous forests and evergreen forests.

When you walk through a deciduous forest in the fall, you can see many leaves on the ground. The leaves have changed from green to red, orange, yellow, or brown. Oak, maple, and elm trees are deciduous trees.

When you walk through an evergreen forest in the fall, there are no needles on the ground. The trees look almost the same all year long. Pine, fir, and spruce trees are evergreen trees.

Some forests have both deciduous trees and evergreen trees in them. What do you think the ground would look like in that kind of forest?

Your Turn!

 Need a Review?
For additional help with context clues, see page 97.

Ready to Try It?
As you read other text, use what you learned about context clues to help you understand it.

Objectives
• Use context clues to figure out the meanings of words you don't know.

Envision It!

Context Clues

Read the words before and after a word that you don't know to help you make sense of it.

I saw a robin, a bluebird, a sapsucker, and a turkey while walking in the woods.

READING STREET ONLINE
VOCABULARY ACTIVITIES
www.ReadingStreet.com

Context Clues

- Context clues are words or sentences near a word you do not know that can help you figure out the meaning of the word.

- When you come to a word you do not know, pause for a moment. Look at the other words in the sentence or in nearby sentences to help you figure out the word's meaning.

- As you read "Nature Hike," look for context clues to help you figure out the meaning of words you don't know.

Nature Hike

Our class went on a nature hike yesterday. Our teacher took us on a walking path through the forest. We learned that the forest is the natural habitat for many kinds of animals.

Animals live in forests for many reasons. There are lots of trees and other plants. This means there is a lot for animals to eat. The trees and plants are also places where animals can build homes and hide from the predators that might eat them.

Our hike was so much fun! We really learned a lot about forests and the animals that live in them.

Your Turn!

 Need a Review?
For additional help with context clues, see page 97.

 Ready to Try It?
As you read other text, use what you learned about context clues to help you understand it.

Antonyms

Antonyms are words that have opposite meaning. *Messy* and *neat* are antonyms.

Messy

Neat

Antonyms can be used to contrast two things. Antonyms help readers understand differences.

Synonyms

Synonyms are words that have the same meaning or similar meaning. *Happy* and *glad* are synonyms.

Happy

Glad

Knowing and using synonyms can help make your writing more interesting. Look in a thesaurus to find synonyms.

Envision It!

Synonyms and Antonyms

- Synonyms are words that have the same or almost the same meaning. *Happy* and *glad* are synonyms.

- Antonyms are words that have opposite meanings. *Messy* and *neat* are antonyms.

- As you read, if you come to a word you don't know, look to see if the author has used a synonym or an antonym. This may help you figure out the word's meaning.

- Look for examples of synonyms and antonyms as you read "My Room."

My Room

My room is always messy, not neat. My mom wants me to clean my room. She says she likes it when my room is orderly.

I like to play with all of my toys at the same time. Sometimes I forget to put my dolls and games away when I am finished playing. When that happens, my room is cluttered and messy. That's when Mom tells me I better go put everything away.

I don't really like to clean, but I like it when my room is tidy.

Your Turn!

❚❚ Need a Review?
For additional help with synonyms and antonyms, see pages 102–103.

▷ Ready to Try It?
As you read other text, use what you learned about synonyms and antonyms to help you understand it.

Envision It!

Synonyms
Synonyms are words that have the same meaning or similar meaning. *Happy* and *glad* are synonyms.

Happy   Glad

Knowing and using synonyms can help make your writing more interesting. Look in a thesaurus to find synonyms.

103

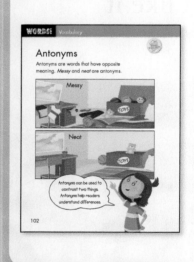

WORDS! Vocabulary

Antonyms
Antonyms are words that have opposite meaning. *Messy* and *neat* are antonyms.

Messy

Neat

Antonyms can be used to contrast two things. Antonyms help readers understand differences.

102

Synonyms and Antonyms

- Synonyms are words that have the same or almost the same meaning. *Neat* and *tidy* are synonyms.

- Antonyms are words that have opposite meanings. *Happy* and *sad* are antonyms.

- As you read, if you come to a word you don't know, look at the words and sentences around it. The author may have used a synonym or antonym. It may help you figure out the meaning of the word you do not know.

- Look for examples of synonyms and antonyms as you read "Cleaning Games."

Cleaning Games

Cleaning your room with a family member can go from unexciting to fun if you make it into a game.

Try playing a game called "Colors." Have your family member pick a color. Pick up all the toys and other articles you can find in that color and put them away neatly. Pick up clothes too!

It is fun to play against brothers and sisters, so why not compete with a sibling? The person who finds the most items of that color and puts them away first wins the race.

It used to be that cleaning your room was dreary, but by making it into a game, it can be exciting!

Your Turn!

 Need a Review?
For additional help with synonyms and antonyms, see pages 102–103.

 Ready to Try It?
As you read other text, use what you learned about synonyms and antonyms to help you understand it.

Prefixes

A prefix is a word part that can be added to the beginning of a base word. In the word *disappear, dis-* is a prefix.

Appear

Disappear

Knowing the meaning of a prefix can help you figure out the meaning of the new word.

Common Prefixes and Their Meanings

un-	not
re-	again, back
in-	not
dis-	not, opposite of
pre-	before

Suffixes

A suffix is a word part added to the end of a base word. In the word *cloudless, -less* is a suffix.

Cloud

Cloudless

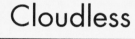

Common Suffixes and Their Meanings

-able	can be done
-ment	action or process
-less	without
-tion	act, process

Knowing how a suffix changes a word can help you figure out the meaning of the new word.

Envision It!

Prefixes and Suffixes

- A prefix is a word part that is added to the beginning of a word. Examples of prefixes are *un-* and *re-*.

- A suffix is a word part that is added to the end of a word. Examples of suffixes are *-ful, -less, -ment,* and *-ly.*

- Prefixes and suffixes change the meanings of words. When you come to a word you don't know, look to see if it has a prefix or a suffix. Prefixes and suffixes can help you figure out the meaning of a word.

My Bike

It was a warm, cloudless day. Uncle Steven and I were going to go on a bike ride, but my bike had a flat tire. I thought the tire was useless.

Uncle Steven said the tire was fixable. There was a hole in the tube inside the tire. He told me that he could patch the tube and reuse it.

After he finished fixing my tire, we went for a ride! One day I will have to repay Uncle Steven for helping me fix my bike!

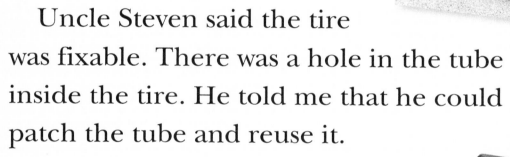

Need a Review?
For additional help with prefixes and suffixes, see pages 108–109.

Ready to Try It?
As you read other text, use what you learned about prefixes and suffixes to help you understand it.

Envision It!

Prefixes and Suffixes

- A prefix is a word part that is added to the beginning of a word. The prefix *pre-*, for example, means "before."

- A suffix is a word part that is added to the end of a word. The suffix *-less*, for example, means "without."

- When you come to a word you don't know, look to see if it has a prefix or a suffix. If you know the meaning of the prefix or suffix, it can help you figure out the meaning of the word.

- Look for prefixes and suffixes as you read "Sunny or Cloudy?"

112

Sunny or Cloudy?

In most places in the United States people get to enjoy all kinds of weather and changes in the seasons. But not all people are in agreement.

For many people, a warm, cloudless day is the best kind of day. There are so many things to do outside. If the weather is unkind and someone has to stay inside, it might feel like punishment.

Other people would disagree. They find cold or rainy weather more enjoyable. When the weather is bad, they can stay inside all day and do other things. They might reread a favorite book or watch a movie.

What's your favorite kind of weather?

Your Turn!

Need a Review?
For additional help with prefixes and suffixes, see pages 108–109.

Ready to Try It?
As you read other text, use what you learned about prefixes and suffixes to help you understand it.

113

Dictionary/Glossary

A dictionary and a glossary both explain the words of our language. Both put the words in alphabetical order. A glossary can be found at the back of a book.

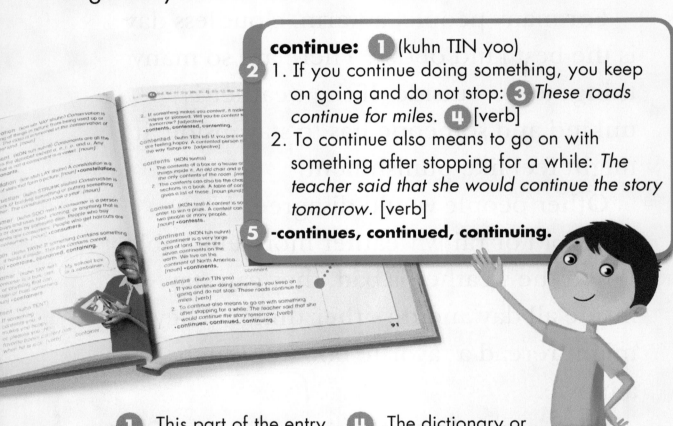

continue: ❶ (kuhn TIN yoo)
❷ 1. If you continue doing something, you keep on going and do not stop: ❸ *These roads continue for miles.* ❹ [verb]
2. To continue also means to go on with something after stopping for a while: *The teacher said that she would continue the story tomorrow.* [verb]
❺ **-continues, continued, continuing.**

❶ This part of the entry shows you how to pronounce the word.

❷ Here is the word's definition.

❸ The word is used in an example to help you understand its meaning.

❹ The dictionary or glossary entry tells you the word's part of speech. *Continue* is a verb.

❺ See how the word changes when an ending is added.

114

Thesaurus

A thesaurus is a book of synonyms. The words in a thesaurus are in alphabetical order.

sleep verb

be asleep, nap, doze, snooze, catch a few z's, take a siesta, catnap

Keep a thesaurus handy when you write. It can help you find just the right word.

Envision It!

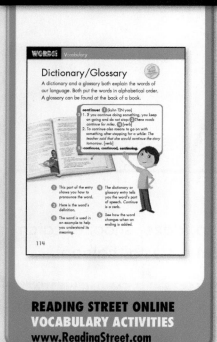

Dictionary and Glossary

- A dictionary is a book that lists words and their meanings. The words are in alphabetical order.

- A glossary is a section at the back of a book that lists words and meanings of words that appear in the book. These words are also in alphabetical order.

- As you read "Sleep," use a dictionary to help you find the meanings of words you do not know.

116

Sleep

Everyone sleeps. Our bodies need sleep to grow and to stay healthy.

Babies need the most sleep. A newborn baby sleeps in a crib or in a bassinette about 13 to 16 hours a day!

The average person sleeps about eight hours every day. That means that we sleep about 122 days every year!

As people get older, they usually spend less time sleeping. People over 70 years old only spend about six hours sleeping each day.

Need a Review?
For additional help using a dictionary or glossary, see page 114.

Ready to Try It?
As you read other text, use a dictionary or glossary to help you understand it.

Objectives

- Understand the purpose of a dictionary. ● Understand the purpose of a glossary.

Envision It!

READING STREET ONLINE
VOCABULARY ACTIVITIES
www.ReadingStreet.com

Dictionary and Glossary

- A dictionary is a book that lists words and their meanings in alphabetical order. A dictionary also shows how to pronounce each word.

- A glossary is also a list of words and their meanings. A glossary appears at the back of a book and lists words that appear in the book. The words are in alphabetical order.

- As you read "Movie Night," use a dictionary to help you find the meanings of words you do not know.

118

Read Together

Movie Night

Last night my brother fell asleep on the couch when he and I were watching television.

We were watching an old movie about a mining town in the 1800s. Lots of people moved to the region from far away. They were trying to find gold. Most of the miners didn't find anything. One man found several large chunks of gold. His discovery was really exciting! He got rich! I really enjoyed watching the movie.

My brother didn't feel the same way. He started snoring after the first few minutes of the movie. Next time we will have to watch something that won't make him doze off!

Your Turn!

❚❚ Need a Review?
For additional help using a dictionary or glossary, see page 114.

▶ Ready to Try It?
As you read other text, use a dictionary or glossary to help you understand it.

Multiple-Meaning Words

Multiple-meaning words are words that can have different meanings depending on how they are used.

Homographs

Homographs are words that are spelled the same. They have different meanings, and they may be pronounced the same way or differently.

Bow

Bow

Read the words before and after a homograph to discover its meaning and pronunciation. Check a dictionary to be sure.

Homonyms

Homonyms are words that are spelled the same. They have different meanings, and they are pronounced the same way.

Pen

You can figure out the meaning of a homonym by reading the words around it.

Pen

Homophones

Homophones are words that sound the same, but they are spelled differently and they have different meanings.

Night

Knight

Homophones might be confusing when you hear them being read aloud. Pay attention to the words before and after the homophone to find its meaning.

Understanding
Homographs, Homonyms, and Homophones

	Pronunciation	Spelling	Meaning
Homographs	may be the same or different	same	different
Homonyms	same	same	different
Homophones	same	different	different

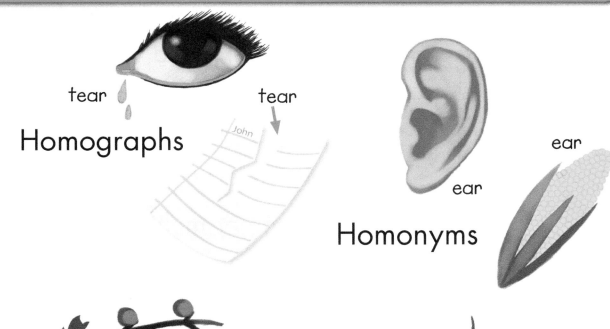

tear

tear

Homographs

ear

ear

Homonyms

berry

Homophones

bury

Objectives

● Distinguish words with multiple meanings and determine which meaning to use.

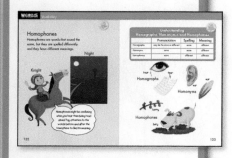

READING STREET ONLINE
VOCABULARY ACTIVITIES
www.ReadingStreet.com

Multiple-Meaning Words

- Multiple-meaning words are words that can have different meanings depending on how they are used. Many multiple-meaning words are spelled and pronounced the same.

- Some multiple-meaning words are spelled the same but pronounced differently.

- Some other multiple-meaning words are spelled differently but pronounced the same.

- Look for examples of multiple-meaning words as you read "The School Play."

The School Play

The night of the school play was so much fun! The play was about King Arthur. I got to play a knight! Sid got to play a knight too. We were the only two knights in the play. I was glad I remembered all my lines.

My friend Danny got to be the king. Elena played the queen. She wore a crown and had a bow in her hair.

At the end of the play, we all got to take a bow. What a fun night!

Your Turn!

⏸ Need a Review?
For additional help with multiple-meaning words, see pages 120–123.

▶ Ready to Try It?
As you read other text, use what you learned about multiple-meaning words to help you understand it.

Envision It!

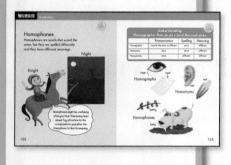

Multiple-Meaning Words

- Multiple-meaning words are words that have more than one definition. Some multiple-meaning words are spelled and pronounced the same way.

- Some other multiple-meaning words are spelled the same way, but they have different pronunciations.

- There are also multiple-meaning words that are spelled differently but pronounced the same way.

- Look for examples of multiple-meaning words as you read "Growing on a Farm."

Growing on a Farm

Many farms have both animals and plants. In the spring, a farmer sows seeds in the fields so that crops can grow. The crops are used to feed people so that they can stay healthy and grow. Some of the crops feed animals. Animals on a farm grow too!

Sows have piglets that will grow up into pigs. Cows have calves that will grow up too!

Ewes have baby sheep that will also grow into adults. When the sheep are older, they can be sheared. When a sheep is sheared, its wool is cut off. We use sheep's wool for many things such as coats and blankets. We also use wool to make socks. Socks keep your feet and calves warm when it is cold.

Your Turn!

❚❚ Need a Review?
For additional help with multiple-meaning words, see pages 120–123.

▶ Ready to Try It?
As you read other text, use what you learned about multiple-meaning words to help you understand it.

Related Words

Related words are words that have the same base word. *Bicycle*, *recycle*, and *cyclone* are related words. They all have the base word *cycle*.

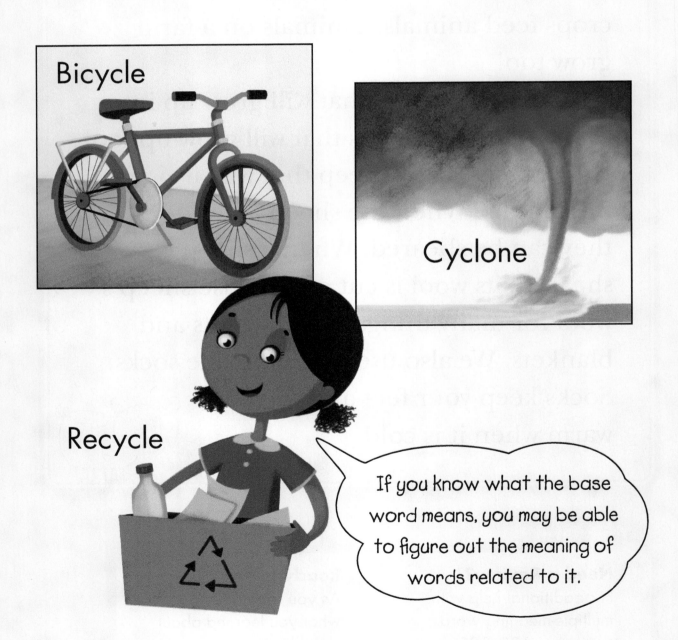

Bicycle

Cyclone

Recycle

If you know what the base word means, you may be able to figure out the meaning of words related to it.

Compound Words

Compound words are words made of two smaller words. *Goldfish* and *basketball* are compound words.

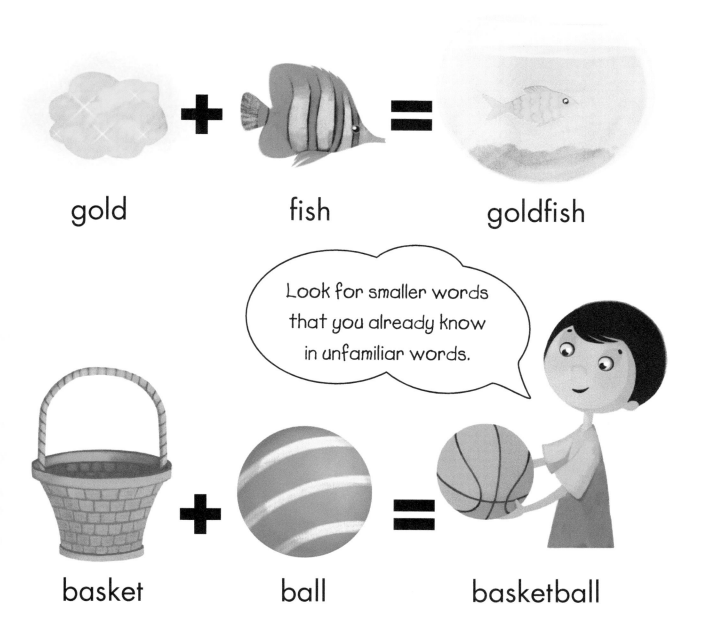

gold + fish = goldfish

Look for smaller words that you already know in unfamiliar words.

basket + ball = basketball

Envision It!

Compound Words

Compound words are words made of two smaller words. *Goldfish* and *basketball* are compound words.

gold + fish = goldfish

Look for smaller words that you already know in unfamiliar words.

basket + ball = basketball

129

READING STREET ONLINE
VOCABULARY ACTIVITIES
www.ReadingStreet.com

Read Together

Compound Words

- A compound word is one word made up of two smaller words.

- You may be able to use the meanings of the smaller words to figure out the meaning of a compound word. For example, a *fishbowl* is a bowl that holds fish.

- Look for compound words as you read "Basketball."

Basketball

Basketball is a team sport. There are five teammates on a team. Unlike football, where teams try to score touchdowns, basketball teams try to score points by putting a ball through a hoop. This is called "making a basket." The team with the most points wins.

Basketball is often played indoors on a basketball court. It can also be played outdoors on a playground or other kind of court.

Basketball is one of the most popular sports in the world. Do boys and girls play this sport in your hometown?

Your Turn!

❚❚ Need a Review?
For additional help with compound words, see page 129.

▶ Ready to Try It?
As you read other text, use what you learned about compound words to help you understand it.

Envision It!

READING STREET ONLINE
VOCABULARY ACTIVITIES
www.ReadingStreet.com

Compound Words

- Compound words are words made up of two smaller words.

- You may be able to use the meanings of the smaller words to figure out the meaning of a compound word. For example, a *raincoat* is a coat that can be worn in the rain.

- Look for compound words as you read "My Day at the Aquarium."

My Day at the Aquarium

My grandpa took me downtown to the city aquarium. The aquarium is so much fun. There are so many different kinds of undersea animals to see.

First, Grandpa and I saw sharks, whales, and dolphins. In another tank there were swordfish, tuna, and sailfish. Then we saw other saltwater animals like starfish, jellyfish, crabs, and eels. Some of them don't look like they are animals at all!

Before we left, we stopped by the gift shop. Grandpa bought me a beautiful seashell to take home. Every time I look at it I will think of our fun day at the aquarium!

Your Turn!

 Need a Review?
For additional help with compound words, see page 129.

 Ready to Try It?
As you read other text, use what you learned about compound words to help you understand it.

133

Envision It! | Genre

Fiction
fable
fairy tale
fantasy
folk tale
informational fiction
realistic fiction

Drama

Poetry

Informational Text
expository text
magazine article
photo essay
procedural text

Literary Nonfiction
autobiography
biography

Let's Think About...

Genre

As you read,
- decide if a story is real or made up.
- ask yourself who the story is about, where it takes place, and what happens.

There are many kinds, or genres, of stories. Knowing a story's genre will help you understand what you read. It can also help you choose other books to read.

Ready to Try It?

Fiction describes imaginary events
or people.

Genre	A **fable** is a short story that teaches a lesson.	A **fairy tale** is a story about imaginary people or places from long ago.
Setting	The time and place can be anytime or anywhere.	The story takes place "once upon a time in a land far away…"
Characters	Animal characters can talk and act like humans.	Characters are sometimes kings, queens, and other royalty.
Plot	A fable can be about anything. Readers relate the lesson to their own lives.	The story has a happy ending.

Genre	A **fantasy** is a story that can't happen in real life.	A **folk tale** is a well-known story that has been told for many years.
Setting	The time and place can be anytime or anywhere.	A folk tale usually takes place "long ago and far away."
Characters	Animals and things may talk or act like people.	Characters are often talking animals. They are usually "good" or "bad."
Plot	The story can be about anything.	A character usually has to solve a problem.

Fiction describes imaginary events or people.

	Informational fiction is a made-up story with a lot of facts.	Realistic fiction is a made-up story that could really happen.
Genre		
Setting	The time and place can be anytime or anywhere.	The setting is in a real place or in a place that seems real.
Characters	Characters can be people or animals. The animals may or may not talk.	Characters are made up but they do real things. There are no talking animals.
Plot	The story might be about science or nature, but it can be about other topics too.	The plot is believable.

Drama and **poetry** tell a real or fictional story in a unique way.

Genre	**Drama** tells a story that is meant to be acted out.	**Poetry** is made up of words put into lines. Poems have rhythm and may rhyme.
Features	There is a list of characters. There are words that describe time and place.	The words of a poem describe the poet's feelings.
Organization	There are lines of dialogue and stage directions.	Not all poems look alike.
Includes...	plays; sketches; scripts; television scripts	free verse poems; songs; funny rhyming poems; poems that tell stories; nursery rhymes

Informational text provides facts, details, and explanations.

Genre	**Expository text** gives facts about real people, animals, places, and events.	A **magazine article** tells information about a topic.
Features	The text is filled with facts. It may have maps, photos, and time lines.	There are facts and details about the topic. Usually there are illustrations.
Organization	The text may tell about events in the order they happen.	Magazines have titles and tables of contents. Articles may have headings.
Includes...	book reports; articles; essays	A magazine article can be about any topic.

Genre	A **photo essay** has many photographs. Words explain the photographs.	**Procedural text** tells how to do something in steps that are easy to follow.
Features	Sentences or paragraphs describe the many photos in detail.	There is a list of things you need. There may be symbols or pictures to help explain.
Organization	Photos are organized in sequence or by category.	There are steps to follow in order. The steps may be numbered.
Includes...	books of photos that tell about a subject, such as farm animals or planets	instructions, such as recipes or rules for a game; how-to articles

Literary nonfiction is narrative text based on facts, real events, and real people.

Genre	An **autobiography** is the true story of a real person's life told by that person.	A **biography** is the true story of a real person's life told by someone else.
Setting	The setting is a real place from the author's life.	The setting is a real place from the person's life.
Characters	The characters are real people from real life.	The characters are real people from real life.
Plot	The plot includes important events in the author's life.	The plot includes important events in the person's life.

I Can Think About...

Fiction

fairy tale

Does the story begin "Once upon a time"?
Are some of the characters kings or queens?

folk tale

Has the story been told for many years?
Are characters either "good" or "bad"?
Does the story remind me of other stories?

fantasy

Are the events in the story make-believe?
Do animals and things act like people?

informational fiction

Where does the story take place?
Is the story filled with facts and details?

realistic fiction

Is the story one that could really happen?
Do characters act like real people?

fable

Do animal characters act like people?
Is there a moral, or lesson?

I Can Think About...
Nonfiction

Read Together

biography
Is this the true story of someone's life?
Are the characters real people from real life?

procedural text
Are there steps that tell me what to do?
Is there a list of things I need?
Are there pictures to help me?

expository text
Are there facts about real people or animals?
Are there facts about real places?
Are there maps, photos, or time lines?

photo essay

Are there a lot of photographs?
Are there words that describe the photos?

autobiography

Is this the true story of someone's life?
Is this written by the person whose life it is about?
Are the characters real people from real life?

magazine article

Are important ideas easy to find?
Are there facts, details, and pictures?
Are there headings?

Read Together

I Can **Think** About...
Drama and Poetry

drama

Is the story meant to be acted out?
Is there a list of characters?
Are there lines that characters speak?

poetry

Is this made up of lines of words?
Is there rhythm, or a beat? Is there rhyme?
Do words describe the author's feelings?

Illustrations

7, 11, 13, 15, 17, 19, 21, 23, 25 Mick Reid
136 Nicole Wong

Photographs

Every effort has been made to secure permission and provide appropriate credit for photographic material. The publisher deeply regrets any omission and pledges to correct errors called to its attention in subsequent editions.

Unless otherwise acknowledged, all photographs are the property of Pearson Education, Inc.

Photo locators denoted as follows: Top (T), Bottom (B), Left (L), Right (R)

49 Digital Vision
59 Digital Vision
69 (T) Getty Images, (B) Jupiter Images
73 American Images Inc/Getty Images
81 David Madison/Getty Images
93 (R) ©AP Images, (L) ©Daniel Dempster Photography/Alamy Images
99 BLOOMimage/Getty Images
101 ©Corbis/SuperStock
131 Stee Satusek/Getty Images
133 Carlos Davilla/Getty Images